Inspiring
Thoughts
on
LIFE

Price: Rs. 95/- (Rupees Ninety five)
Edition : 2007 © Rajpal & Sons
ISBN - 978 - 81 - 7028 - 714 - 8
Inspiring Thoughts on Life

Rajpal & Sons
Madarsa Road, Kashmere Gate, Delhi-110006
www.rajpalsons.com

$\mathcal{I}$nspiring
Thoughts
on
LIFE

Edited by **Meera Johri**

rajpal

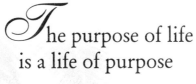

$\mathcal{T}$he purpose of life
is a life of purpose

Robert Byrne

$\mathcal{I}$f a man hasn't
discovered something that
he will die for
he isn't fit to live

Martin Luther King

$\mathscr{E}$njoy the little things
for one day you may look
back and realise
they were the big things

Robert Brault

People are lonely
because they build
walls
instead of
bridges

Anonymous

8

*D*on't be afraid
of going slowly
Be afraid
of standing still

❧

Japanese proverb

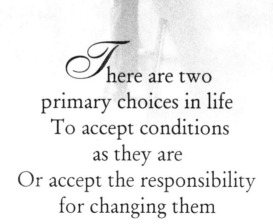

$\mathcal{T}$here are two
primary choices in life
To accept conditions
as they are
Or accept the responsibility
for changing them

Denis Waitley

$\mathcal{W}$e worry about what
a child will become
tomorrow
yet we forget
that he is someone today

Stacia Tauscher

11

The miracle is not
to fly in the air
or to walk on the water
but
to walk on the earth

Chinese proverb

*I*n matters of style
swim with the current
In matters of principle
stand like a rock

Thomas Jefferson

The foolish man seeks
happiness in the distance
the wise
grows it under his feet

James Oppenheim

*I*f you want to earn more
learn more
If you want to get more
out of the world
you must put
more into the world
For after all
men will get no more out of life
than
they put into it

William Roetcker

$\mathscr{M}$en are not
prisoners of fate
but only prisoners
of their own minds

Franklin D Roosevelt

$\mathcal{I}$t is the friends you
can call up
at four in the morning
that matter

❧

Marlene Dietrich

$\mathscr{T}$hat what you really believe
in always happens
And the belief in a thing
makes it happen

Frank Llyod Wright

*T*each the young
people how to think
and not
what to think

∾

Sydney Sugarman

The firsts go away
first love
first baby
first kiss
You have to create new ones

Sarah Jessica Parker

$\mathcal{L}$ive every day
like it's your last
cause one day
you're gonna be right

Ray Charles

$\mathcal{E}$ndure today's pain today
Do not add it to yesterday's
nor attempt to shoulder
tomorrow's

∾

Aureliano Tapia Mendez

$\mathcal{T}$he mighty oak was
once just a small nut
who stood his ground

Rianna Nadon

$\mathcal{C}$ynics always say no
Saying yes
leads to knowledge
So for as long as
you have the strength to
say yes

∾

Stephen Colbert

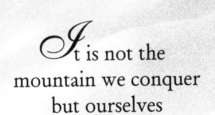

*I*t is not the
mountain we conquer
but ourselves

Sir Edmund Hillary

*W*herever you go
go with all your heart

Confucius

$\mathcal{D}$o not go
where the path may lead
go where there is no
path and leave a trail

❧

Ralph Waldo Emerson

You have to do the right thing...
You may never know what
results come from your actions
But if you do nothing
there will be no results

Mahatma Gandhi

Every child is an artist
The problem is
how to remain an artist
once he grows up

Pablo Picasso

$\mathcal{G}$ratitude unlocks the
fullness of life
It turns what we have
into enough and more...
It can turn
a meal into a feast
a house into a home
a stranger into a friend

Melodie Beattie

I always
do things I can't do
that's how
I get to do them

❧

Pablo Picasso

$\mathscr{A}$ child is not
a vase to be filled
but
a fire to be lit

Rabelias

*D*o not pray for easy lives
Pray to be stronger men

Phillips Brooks

$\mathcal{I}$'ve never believed
in measuring one's worth by the
size of his or her bank account
I prefer to look at
the distance travelled

Dan Rather

There is no need for temples
no need for complicated philosophy
Our own brain
our own heart
is our temple
the philosophy is kindness

Dalai Lama

$\mathcal{D}$on't wait for the Last Judgement
It is taking place everyday

Albert Camus

*W*e can easily forgive
a child who is
afraid of the dark
The real tragedy of life
is when people are
afraid of the light

Plato

The secret of
what life's all about
was answered by the sages
Life's all about
one day at a time
no matter
what your age is

Robert Half

$\mathscr{I}$t is not
because things are difficult
that we do not dare
It is because
we do not dare
that things are difficult

Seneca

*P*ain is temporary
It may last a minute or
an hour or a day or a year
But eventually it will subside
and something else will
take its place..
If I quit
however
it lasts forever

❧

Lance Armstrong

*I*mpossible is just a big word
thrown around by small men
who find it easier to live
in the world they've been given
than to explore the power
they've been given
to change it
Impossible is not a fact
Impossible is not a declaration
It's a dare
Impossible is potential
Impossible is temporary
Impossible is nothing

An Adidas Advertisement

*W*e don't see
things as they are
We see them
as we are

∞

Anais Nin

$\mathcal{E}$veryone is kneaded
out of the same dough
but not baked
in the same oven

Yiddish proverb

$\mathcal{H}$ope is like
a road in the country
There was never a road
but when
many people walk on it
the road
comes into existence

❧

LinYutang

*N*obody trips over mountains
It is the small pebble
that causes you to stumble
Pass all the pebbles
in your path
and you will find that
you have crossed the mountain

Josh Billings

*H*ave a time and place
for everything
and do everything
in it's time and place
And you will not only
accomplish more
but have far more leisure
than those who are always hurrying
as if vainly attempting
to overtake time
that had been lost

Tryon Edwards

$\mathcal{A}$ lot of people are afraid
to say what they want
That's why they don't
get what they want

Madonna

The charm of a deed
is its doing
the charm of a life
is its living
the soul of the thing
is the thought

Eugene Fitchware

$\mathcal{T}$here are two things
to aim for in life
first, to get what you want
and after that to enjoy it
Only the wisest of mankind
achieve the second

❧

Logan Pearsall Smith

$\mathcal{T}$he important thing
is this
to be able at any moment
to sacrifice what we are
for what we could become

✵

Charles Du Bois

*P*ut all good eggs in one basket
and then
watch that basket

Andrew Carnegie

*T*ime cannot be
influenced by mankind
It gives each of us
a beginning and an end
And this makes us
question the signifigance of
what comes in between
But if you can create
something time cannot erode
something which ignores the
eccentrities of particular
eras or moments
something truly timeless
this is a significant victory

Ferdinando Porsche

*H*ealth is a precious thing
and the only one meriting
that a man should lay out
not only his
time, sweat, labour and goods
but also
life itself to obtain it

Michel De Montaigne

I am only one
I cannot do everything
But still I can do something
And I will not refuse to do
the something
I can do

Helen Keller

The art of living
does not consist
in preserving and clinging
to a particular mood of
happiness
but in allowing happiness
to change its form
without being
disappointed by the change
For happiness
like a child
must be allowed to grow up

Charles Morgan

$\mathcal{I}$t is not easy to find
happiness in ourselves
and it is not possible
to find it elsewhere

❧

Agnes Repplier

$\mathcal{L}$ook within for value
and
look beyond for perspective

Denis Waitley

$\mathcal{T}$he more you praise and
celebrate your life
the more there is in life to
celebrate

Oprah Winfrey

You can't help getting older but you don't have to get old

George Burns

*I*t is a terrible thing
to see
and
have no vision

Helen Keller

A truly good book
teaches me better
than to merely read it
I must soon lay it down and
commence living on its hint
What I began by reading
I must finish by acting

Henry David Thoreau

*T*ruth
is the highest virtue
but higher still
is truthful living

❧

Guru Nanak

What you have inherited
from your fathers
earn over again for yourselves
or it will not be yours

Goethe

$\mathcal{H}$ave a good laugh everyday
even if the situation is ridiculous

Anthony B Montapert

Do not spoil what you
have by desiring
what you have not
Remember
that what you now have
was once among the things
you only hoped for

Epicurus

*T*hought is only a flash
between
two long nights
But
this flash
is everything

Henri Poincare

Joy is neither happiness nor sorrow
Joy is purity of mind
When the sky is clear and quiet
then it is said to be joyful
When there is neither
the desire of gain
nor the storm of loss
then it is called happiness
The constant practice should be
to remain joyful
in all circumstances

∽

Acharya Mahaprajna

$\mathscr{B}$elieve nothing
merely because you have been told it
or because it is traditional
or because
you yourself have imagined it
Do not believe
what your teacher tells you merely
out of respect for the teacher
But whatever
after due examination and analysis
you find to be conducive
to the good
the benefit
the welfare of all beings
that doctrine believe and cling to
and take it as your guide

❧

Buddha

$\mathcal{W}$hat's the difference
between
school and life?
In school
you're taught a lesson
and then given a test
In life
you're given a test
that teaches you a lesson

Anonymous

*N*othing is all wrong
Even a clock
that has stopped running
is right twice a day
Patience is
the ability to
let your light shine
after your fuse has blown

❧

Anonymous

$\mathcal{S}$ubdue your appetites
and you have
conquered human nature

&

Charles Dickens

*H*ard work
spotlights
the characater of people
Some turn up their sleeves
some turn up their noses
and
some don't turn up at all

Sam Ewig

$\mathcal{O}$ur lives begin to end
the day we start
being silent
about the things that matter

Martin Luther King

$\mathcal{D}$on't
compromise yourself
You
are all you've got

Janis Joplin

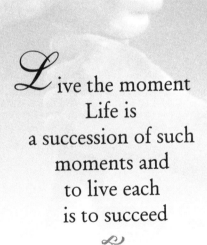

$\mathscr{L}$ive the moment
Life is
a succession of such
moments and
to live each
is to succeed

Corita Kent

$\mathscr{N}$ever stand begging
for what you have
the power to earn

Miguel de Cervantes

A

'No'
uttered from deepest conviction
is better and greater
than a
'Yes'
uttered to please
or worse
to avoid trouble

Mahatma Gandhi

$\mathcal{D}$on't be afraid to take
a big step
You can't cross a chasm
in
two
small
jumps

❧

David Uyod George

$\mathcal{T}$he art of becoming
wise is the art of
knowing what to overlook

William James

I now know that a
good mind must be
flexible and open to change
The older I get
the more I realize
that
there are few absolutes
and
many perspectives

❧

Susan Brownmiller

$\mathcal{W}$e ask ourselves
who am I to be
brilliant, gorgeous, talented, fabulous?
Actually
who are you not to be?

Mariannae

81

$\mathscr{D}$rop the question
what tomorrow may bring
and
count as profit
everyday that fate allows you

Horace

$\mathscr{E}$njoyment is not a goal
It is a feeling
that accompanies
important ongoing activity

Paul Goodman

$\mathcal{Y}$ou don't get anything
clean without getting
something else
dirty

Cecil Baxter

$\mathcal{T}$o gain
that which is worth having
it maybe necessary
to lose everything

Bernadette Davlin

$\mathcal{I}$t doesn't matter
who you love
or what you love
but
that you love

❧

Michael Dougles

*C*hase your passion
not your pension

Daisaku Ikeda

*E*very moment
we are changing fate
according to
the thoughts we think

William James

$\mathcal{G}$od does not require us
to succeed
He only requires us
to try

Mother Teresa

$\mathcal{I}$t's easy to make
a buck
It's a lot tougher to make
a difference

❧

Tom Brokaw

$\mathcal{M}$y sorrows
my hurts
don't stay with me
because I am very optimistic
and forgive easily
If your hurt stays
it brings about your downfall

Dev Anand

The knowledge is very
superficial which remains
only on your tongue
The intrinsic merit and value
of knowledge is
that you act upto it

Nahjul Balaga - Saying 90

Do more than exist ... live
Do more than touch ... feel
Do more than look ... observe
Do more than read ... absorb
Do more than hear ... listen
Do more than listen ... understand

John H Rhodes

You have to learn the
rules of the game
And then you have to play
better than anyone else

❧

Albert Einstein

*I*t's good to have
money and the things
that money can buy
But it's good, too,
to check up once in a while
and make sure that
you haven't lost the things
that money can't buy

❧

George H Lorimer

$\mathcal{W}$ork is a slice of your life
It's not the entire pizza

Jacquelyn Mitchard

$\mathcal{N}$ot everything that
can be counted counts
And not everything
that counts
can be counted

℘

Albert Einstein

There are only
two lasting bequests
we can hope to give our children
One is roots
the other, wings

Hodding Carter

A bird doesn't sing
because it has an answer
It sings
because it has a song

Maya Angelou

$\mathcal{Y}$ou don't get to choose
how you're going to die or when
You can only decide
how you're going to live now

Joan Baez

$\mathcal{N}$ever doubt that
a small group of
thoughtful committed citizens
can change the world
Indeed
it is the only thing
that ever has

Margaret Mead

*Stop worrying
about the potholes in the road
and
celebrate
the journey*

≈

Barbara Hoffman

$\mathcal{M}$ake it a point
to do something every day that
you don't want to do
This is the golden rule for
acquiring the habit of
doing your duty without pain

Mark Twain

*W*hen all's said and done
all roads lead to the same end
So it's not so much
which road you take
as how you take it

Charles de Lint